ABRAHAM LINCOLN

LARRY METZGER

ABRAHAM
LINCOLN

FRANKLIN WATTS
NEW YORK / LONDON / TORONTO / SYDNEY
A FIRST BOOK / 1987

Cover photograph courtesy of The Granger Collection, New York.

Photographs courtesy of: The Collections of the Library of Congress:
pp. 12, 15, 23, 24, 27, 49, 54, 57, 60, 65. 68, 69, 71, 72, 74, 75,
81, 85, 86; New York Public Library Picture Collection: p. 77.

Library of Congress Cataloging-in-Publication Data

Metzger, Larry.
Abraham Lincoln.

(A First book)
Bibliography: p.
Includes index.
Summary: Follows the life of America's sixteenth
president, with an emphasis on his personal life and
early career as lawyer, lawmaker, and abolitionist.
1. Lincoln, Abraham, 1809-1865—Political career
before 1861—Juvenile literature.   2. Presidents—
United States—Biography—Juvenile literature.
[1. Lincoln, Abraham, 1809-1865.   2. Presidents]
I. Title.
E457.905.M48   1987   973'.092'2   [B]   86-22455
ISBN 0-531-10307-2

CONTENTS

Chapter One
"Abraham Lincoln Is My Name"
11

Chapter Two
A Frontier Childhood
20

Chapter Three
On His Own
33

Chapter Four
Courtship and Marriage
40

Chapter Five
"A House Divided Against Itself"
47

Chapter Six
Hard Choices
53

Chapter Seven
The Long Struggle
64

Chapter Eight
Victory and Death
79

For Further Reading
89

Index
91

To Elizabeth

ABRAHAM LINCOLN

"ABRAHAM LINCOLN
IS MY NAME"

1

What an odd child Abraham Lincoln was!

One day, shortly after his eighth birthday, a flock of wild geese flew over the Lincoln cabin. Nobody was surprised when Abraham aimed a gun through the doorway and shot one of the birds. He should have been proud of himself. After all, it was wintertime, and his family needed the food. But Abraham was sad. He loved animals and felt bad about killing the goose. Abraham's father did not understand his son's feelings.

Most boys Abraham's age would have been thrilled by their first hunting success.

As he grew older, Abraham continued to show signs of being peculiar. When he was about eleven or twelve, he wrote a poem about himself:

Abraham Lincoln
his hand and pen

he will be good but
god knows when

Abraham Lincoln is my nam[e]
And with my pen I wrote the same
I wrote in both hast[e] and speed
and left it here for fools to read.

Pioneer boys were not supposed to write poetry. In fact, many pioneers could not read or write.

Today we would not think there was anything unusual about a boy who wrote poems and disliked killing animals. After all, few of us hunt for food any more, and many of us learn to write poetry in school. But Abraham Lincoln grew up in a different time and place, and in his world, he was a strange boy.

Abraham was born in Kentucky in 1809. At that time the United States was much smaller than it is today. It did not yet extend all the way to the Pacific Ocean, and it had a population of only 7,200,000 people. (There are over 230,000,000 people in the United States today.) In the early 1800s, cities were small and there were few factories. As a result, most Americans lived in the countryside and were farmers.

At this time there were still slaves in the United States. Most of them lived in the South and all of them were black. In fact, in 1809, one out of every five Americans was a slave.

The statue of Lincoln
at the Lincoln Memorial
in Washington, D.C.

Kentucky was a slave state. It was also part of the frontier, an area that was covered with forests and where Indians and white pioneers lived. Pioneer farmers, like the Lincolns, had to produce most of what they needed for themselves. They grew all of their own food and made their own clothes, furniture, and tools.

Abraham's parents, Thomas and Nancy Hanks Lincoln, were typical pioneers. They were poor, they were farmers, and they could not read or write. When Thomas was only sixteen years old, his father was killed by an Indian. After that, Thomas had to work to help support himself, his mother, and two sisters. He never made much money. Pioneer life was difficult, and like many women, Nancy Lincoln aged very quickly. When she was still fairly young, she lost most of her teeth.

One of Abraham's first memories was of a close escape from death. He was a small boy at the time and had either jumped or fallen into a stream near his family's log cabin. He tried desperately to keep himself afloat, but he did not know how to swim.

If Abraham had drowned, his death would not have been unusual. Many children on the frontier did not survive. Abraham Lincoln, though, was one of the lucky ones. A neighbor who happened to be nearby jumped into the stream and rescued him.

When he was growing up, Abraham Lincoln wore deerskin pants and shirts and raccoon fur hats. He ate foods like boiled cabbage, bacon, pork, deer, and cornbread. Even this simple diet was not easy to come by. Before any farming could begin, pioneers had to cut down trees, plow the land, and plant seeds. Sometimes the crops didn't grow because the farmers didn't plant the seeds correctly or be-

The birthplace and home of Lincoln

cause the soil was poor. At other times, droughts or storms destroyed the harvest. When these things happened, a pioneer family could easily starve to death.

One of Abraham's early memories shows how hard it was to farm on the frontier. One day when he was still a very young boy, Abraham went out into the fields to help his father plant pumpkins. After Thomas Lincoln loosened the soil with a hoe, Abraham followed and dropped seeds into the ground. Abraham was proud of being able to help his father. Then, a few days later, their work was suddenly ruined. A violent thunderstorm caused a flood that washed away all of the pumpkin seeds and all of the Lincolns' corn, as well. The family had to work very hard to replace the lost crops.

In the winter of 1815–1816, when Abraham was about seven years old, he went to school for the first time. It might seem odd that he started school at the harshest time of the year, but during the other seasons he was needed at home to help with the chores. During the winter there was not much farm work to be done.

Abraham and his older sister, Sarah, had to walk a long distance through the snowy woods to get to the school, which was quite different from our schools today. It was a one-room log building with one teacher for students of all ages. The children studied their lessons by reading out loud so that the teacher could tell who was really working. Anybody who misbehaved was hit with a rod. Abraham probably felt the rod often, because by this time he was a mischievous little boy.

In 1816, the Lincolns moved north to the territory of Indiana. Abraham did not know exactly why the family was leaving Kentucky. There was some kind of a dispute over who really owned his father's land, but Abraham did not understand what it was all about. His father also said something about wanting to live in a place where there were no slaves (slavery was illegal in Indiana). It was all very confusing to Abraham.

In the fall, the Lincolns packed all their belongings and began the trip to their new home. Moving on the frontier was a difficult business. The Lincolns walked the entire way, because they carried things like pots, pans, and a spinning wheel on their horses and in their wagon.

They traveled over 100 miles (160 km) on foot, crossing the mighty Ohio River and cutting their way through the heavy forest on the other side. Abraham helped clear a path by chopping through grapevines and heavy underbrush with an ax. Years later, he remembered the trip to Indiana as one of the hardest things he had ever done.

Winter was a bad time to be settling into a new home in the wilderness. Food was hard to come by, because the local farmers had harvested all their crops and the wild berries had all been picked. The Lincolns also had to build some kind of shelter quickly or they would have frozen to death.

The family immediately put up a temporary hut called a "half-faced cabin," which was actually a kind of lean-to built out of wood, mud, and grass. They kept a fire burning constantly on the open side and wrapped themselves in furs for extra warmth. In this uncomfortable home, they shivered their way through the first few weeks at Pigeon Creek.

Fortunately, the Lincolns did not have to spend their entire winter this way. Thomas was a skilled carpenter who had built several cabins before, and Abraham was able to help by clearing brush and by trimming branches from the logs that were used to make the cabin walls. Furthermore, the Lincolns' neighbors gave them a hand, because it was the custom in pioneer communities to help new families get settled. As a result, a few days after Abraham's eighth birthday, the Lincolns moved into their new house.

This cabin was not very comfortable either. It had a dirt floor and log walls. The Lincolns heated their home by burning wood in a stone fireplace, and they filled the spaces between the logs with mud and grass in order to keep out the wind. The rain often washed away this mortar, though, so the house was always drafty. Abraham slept in the attic, which had a leaky roof.

When spring came that year, it was time for the family to clear the trees and brush so they could start a farm. This was hard work, because the land was heavily wooded and they had only axes to do the job. Even though Abraham was only eight years old, he helped his father chop down trees and split logs for firewood and fence rails.

After they cleared the land, Abraham and his father plowed the soil and planted corn. When the corn ripened, Abraham helped to harvest it and carry it to the mill, where it was ground into flour.

Later that year, Nancy Lincoln's nineteen-year-old cousin, Dennis Hanks, and her Aunt Elizabeth and Uncle Thomas Sparrow moved to Pigeon Creek. Even though Dennis was much older than Abraham, the two boys became close friends.

The Lincolns did not have much time to enjoy their new companions, because in the summer of 1818, an epidemic of "milk sick" broke out at Pigeon Creek. "Milk sick" was an illness that people got from drinking the milk of cows that had eaten a poisonous plant called snakeroot. Many of the settlers, including the Sparrows, died from "milk sick" that summer. Dennis Hanks survived and moved into the Lincoln cabin, where he and Abraham now shared the attic sleeping quarters.

Then, in the fall, Nancy came down with the illness. In October, she died. Thomas Lincoln built a coffin for his wife and, on a windy autumn day, Abraham watched as his mother was buried. He was nine years old.

A FRONTIER
CHILDHOOD

—2—

After Nancy Lincoln's death, Abraham's sister, Sarah, tried to run the household. This had been hard work for Nancy and, for eleven-year-old Sarah, it was impossible. Pioneer women did hard physical labor. The job of cleaning a log cabin with a dirt floor was difficult enough, but Sarah had many other regular chores. She had to cook meals in the fireplace and she had to make, repair, and clean clothes for four people by hand.

Sarah tried to replace her mother, but the job was too much for her. After about a year, the little cabin at Pigeon Creek became a dirty and depressing place. On top of these troubles, in 1819, Abraham was badly injured when a horse kicked him in the head. For a while, his family was afraid that he would die.

After the harvest that year, Thomas Lincoln mysteriously left the family for a trip back to Kentucky. Abraham and Sarah wondered why their father had gone off, but he did not tell them the reason for his trip. While he was gone, the children were left to fend for themselves.

Abraham and Sarah were surprised when their father returned a few months later with a new wife, a widow named Sally Johnston. Sally also had three young children. Suddenly, Abraham had a new mother, a new brother, and two new sisters.

Even though there were now eight people crowded into the cabin, Thomas's marriage to Sally Johnston improved life for the Lincoln family. There were more people to help with the household and farming chores, and Sally made the house a more pleasant place. From Kentucky she brought such luxuries as a clothes chest, a table and chairs, knives, forks, spoons, and, most amazing, a soft feather mattress! Sally also persuaded Thomas to put in a wood floor, whitewash the ceiling, and repair the roof so that snow and rain would no longer leak in on Abraham and Dennis Hanks when they were sleeping in the attic.

Abraham came to prefer his stepmother to his father. Sally was firm with the children, but she was also kindhearted and cheerful and she appreciated Abraham's sense of humor. One day Abraham brought a small boy into the cabin and lifted the child up so that he could make muddy footprints across the freshly painted ceiling. When Sally saw the mess, she did not get angry. Instead, she joined the boys in laughing about the joke. But Abraham had to repaint the ceiling.

During the next few winters Abraham attended school again. By this time, he was growing so rapidly that his pants were often 6 inches (15 cm) too short. At the new school Abraham studied reading, writing, and arithmetic. The lessons were boring, but he was curious and eager to learn.

It was hard for Abraham to do his homework at night, because the only light in the house came from the fireplace. Paper was difficult to get, so he practiced his writing and arithmetic on a wooden shovel in front of the fire. When the shovel was covered, he shaved off a layer of wood and started again. Sometimes he even wrote in the dust or snow. Abraham's handwriting became so good that his family and neighbors often asked him to compose letters for them.

Abraham loved to read, but books were hard to come by on the frontier. The Lincolns did not own any books, so Abraham was forced to borrow. He read everything he could get his hands on, and he read his favorites many times. He brought books into the fields when he was plowing, and he read them whenever he stopped to eat lunch or to let the horses rest. Abraham loved reading so much that he even read *Dilworth's Spelling Book*!

But his favorite book was the *Life of Washington*, by Parson Weems. This was the story of George Washington, the first president of the United States. Abraham was particularly interested in the battles fought by Washington's armies against the British during the American Revolution. He was so excited by the descriptions of these battles that he was able to imagine the smell of gunpowder and the sounds of cannons and muskets as he read. George Washington became one of Abraham's heroes.

Abraham seemed to be interested in almost everything that went on around him. When friends came to visit his parents, he listened quietly while the grown-ups talked. But when the visitors left, he asked Thomas and Sally question after question until he understood everything that had been discussed. Then Abraham repeated the conversation over

As a young boy, Lincoln loved to read.

and over again so that he would not forget what had been said.

As Abraham grew older, his curiosity increased. He often went to the local blacksmith shop and to Gentry's store so he could listen to people tell stories and have discussions. Abraham also enjoyed hearing lawyers argue legal cases. He liked this so much that he and his cousin, Dennis, often walked 15 miles (24 km) to the nearest courthouse to listen to a good trial. After all, a robbery or murder case could be an exciting mystery story!

At the age of fourteen, Abraham began to work for wages in order to bring more money into the family. When a church was built near Pigeon Creek, he became its caretaker, which meant that he was responsible for sweeping the floor, filling the woodbox, and checking the candle supply.

Abraham also did work for local farmers, and he soon became famous for his skill as an axman. One of his neighbors said, "If you heard him felling trees in a clearing, you would say there were three men at work the way the trees fell." Yet Abraham was beginning to discover that he did not enjoy hard physical labor. He preferred to spend his time sitting under a tree, reading a good book. Some people thought he was lazy or even a little strange.

The hard work did not seem to have hurt Abraham, because by the time he was sixteen he had grown to be over 6 feet (183 cm) tall. Although he looked awkward, he was one of the fastest runners and best wrestlers in the

Lincoln was a skilled axman.

neighborhood. And he was very strong—so strong that he could grab an ax by the handle and hold it straight out from his body.

Because he was athletic, friendly, and good at telling stories and jokes, Abraham was popular with the other boys. But he was shy around girls. Perhaps this was because of his appearance. He was skinny and had dark eyes and hair that never stayed combed. Even though he was a good athlete, the girls his age thought he was clumsy and homely, so they made fun of him. Their teasing hurt his feelings and made him even more shy.

When he was seventeen, Abraham left home for the first time to work on a ferry that took people across the Ohio River between Indiana and Kentucky. He was a young man now, and this was an exciting job, offering him many new sights and experiences. He encountered strange and outlandish people—the hunters, gamblers, and traders who traveled along the river. They were tough men who carried guns and brawled constantly, but who also seemed to have lives filled with adventure.

As interesting as the people, however, were the steamboats that Abraham saw traveling up and down the river, spewing soot and ash from their tall smokestacks. These were amazing machines—boats that moved without the aid of sails or oars. Abraham wondered what propelled these strange vessels.

When the ferry job ended, Abraham went back to Pigeon Creek with a growing desire to see more of the

Mr. Lincoln as a ferryman

world. He quickly realized that he was no longer happy at home. He and his father were not getting along. In many ways, Thomas Lincoln was proud of his son. Abraham was a hard worker and he was obviously smart. But there was a great deal about him that made no sense to Thomas. Thomas could not understand why Abraham spent so much time doing silly things like reading and writing poetry. On his part, Abraham was embarrassed that his father was so uneducated.

Abraham was also becoming ambitious. His books and his job at the ferry had convinced him that there was more to life than farming in the Indiana wilderness. He was determined not to remain a poor pioneer like his father.

Fortunately for Abraham, changes in America at that time were creating new opportunities for ambitious young men. In the Midwest, where the Lincolns lived, farmers were now able to produce more food than their own families needed. The farmers needed places to sell their surpluses, which is why men started general stores like the one owned by James Gentry near Pigeon Creek. Thomas Lincoln and other farmers could sell their extra corn and pork to Mr. Gentry in return for tools and clothing that the storekeeper had bought from eastern factories.

Once Mr. Gentry had bought all that pork and corn, though, he had a problem. He wanted to sell the food to people in the eastern factory towns, but in the 1820s it was not easy to ship things across the country. Because there were no railroads or highways, goods had to be transported by boat along the great rivers. This is what gave Abraham his chance to get away from home and see a bit more of the world.

In April 1828, Abraham Lincoln agreed to take a boatload of farm products for James Gentry down the Ohio and Mississippi rivers to the city of New Orleans. He was nineteen years old at the time and accompanied by Mr. Gentry's son, Allen.

This was a trip of 1,200 miles (1,930 km), and it was a great adventure. Abraham and Allen traveled on a flatboat, which was a vessel unlike any that sails on the Mississippi River today. It was a raft made out of logs and was about 65 feet (20 m) long and 18 feet (5.5 m) wide (the size of a small house). In the middle was a cabin to protect the two young men from bad weather.

Along the way Abraham and Allen had to be wary of many dangers. The Ohio River was quiet and peaceful enough, but the Mississippi was another story. Because of its swift current and its many sandbars and half-sunken tree trunks, boatmen called it the "wicked river." As the two young men guided their raft downstream, they saw the wrecks of other boats that had run aground on the underwater hazards. It took great skill to handle a flatboat on the Mississippi River.

While traveling south along the river, Abraham and Allen began to notice that the climate and the countryside were changing. They could feel the air become warmer and more humid. They could see new types of plants, such as trees with moss hanging from their branches. Abraham and Allen also saw farms that were different from the homesteads of Indiana. The southern farms were plantations where black slaves did the hard labor of growing sugar, cotton, and tobacco. Near the city of Baton Rouge, Louisiana, Abraham and Allen stopped at one of these plantations and traded part of their cargo for some cotton, sugar, and tobacco.

A few nights later, they tied up their flatboat near another plantation. As the young men were resting, seven slaves attacked them. Abraham never knew why. Perhaps the slaves had hoped to take the boat and escape from their master. In the fierce fight that followed, both Abraham and Allen were hurt, but they were able to drive off their attackers. It had been a terrifying experience, so they hauled in their anchor and headed downstream as quickly as possible.

Soon Abraham and Allen reached their destination—New Orleans, at the mouth of the Mississippi, near the Gulf of Mexico. Abraham was absolutely amazed by New Orleans. He had never before been in a town of more than 150 people. New Orleans was a great city—the fifth largest in the United States at the time—with a population of about 30,000. Most of Abraham's friends and neighbors in Indiana were farmers, shopkeepers, and tradesmen who dressed in rough jeans or deerskins and lived in log cabins. In New Orleans Abraham saw wealthy plantation owners and merchants who lived in great mansions and wore fine silk and cotton clothing. He also heard strange new languages like French and Spanish.

Along the waterfront he saw over 1,000 flatboats from the North, as well as great ocean-going sailing vessels being loaded with goods that would be shipped to the eastern cities of the United States or to other parts of the world.

Abraham and Allen quickly sold their cargo and spent a few days taking in the wonders of the city. Abraham enjoyed most of his tour, but he was disturbed by one thing—the slave market, where black people in chains were bought and sold by plantation owners and slave traders. This was different from Abraham's first experience with slaves. The night his boat had been attacked on the river, he had seen them only as enemies to be driven away. Now he saw slaves as human beings who were being treated like cattle, and it made him angry.

After a few days in New Orleans, it was time for Abraham and Allen to return home, but they did not travel back the same way they came. Moving north against the strong current of the Mississippi River on a flatboat would take four months of hard work, so they sold their raft for firewood and sailed upstream on a steamboat. Even this could be an adventure, because steamboats were not very safe at this time. They frequently burned as a result of boiler explosions or sank after snagging on underwater logs. Abraham and Allen were lucky, though, and they finally arrived home in Indiana three months after the start of their journey. Abraham had made twenty-five dollars, and he turned almost all of it over to his father, who had the right to collect his earnings until Abraham reached the age of twenty-one.

Abraham now went back to working for his father, but the trip (and perhaps the loss of twenty-five dollars) increased his discontent with the dull routine of farm life.

Two years later, he got an opportunity to set out on his own. In March 1830 his father decided to move the family to Illinois, because a relative had sent them a glowing description of the state. That spring the Lincolns built some wagons, sold their farm, and set out on the journey to their new home. Abraham, who was twenty-one years old, did not have to go with his family because he was now legally an adult. He went along, however, because he hoped to find a more interesting life in Illinois.

The Lincolns settled in the center of the state in an area

that was very different from the forests of Indiana. Central Illinois was a flat, empty, windy land called the prairie. After the Lincolns arrived, Abraham helped his father build another cabin, clear the rough prairie grass off ten acres, plant corn, and split logs for fence rails.

By the end of the summer, the family had gotten off to a good start in their new home. They had a house and plenty of food. In the autumn, though, things became much more difficult. The entire family came down with malaria, a disease that brought high fevers and "the shakes."

This was followed by one of the worst winters that anybody could remember—the winter of "deep snow." It began when a blizzard struck in December. Over three feet of snow fell. Then came high winds that blew the snow into huge drifts. The temperature stayed below 0°F (—18°C) for much of the next two months. While settlers were trapped in their cabins, many animals froze to death outside.

Somehow, the Lincolns survived. When spring finally arrived and the snow melted, Thomas and Sally Lincoln moved again, but this time Abraham did not go with them. He had decided to set out on his own.

ON HIS OWN

3

During the winter of "deep snow," Abraham and his cousin Dennis Hanks had become friendly with a local businessman named Denton Offutt. Mr. Offutt had offered to pay them to take a flatboat of goods to New Orleans. This seemed like a good opportunity to travel, so Abraham and his cousin accepted the job. They decided to take Abraham's stepbrother, John Johnston, with them. Thus, when Thomas and Sally Lincoln moved in the spring, Abraham, Dennis Hanks, and John Johnston stayed behind to build a flatboat. It took them four weeks to complete the boat.

This first part of their trip took them down the Sangamon River. They had an easy time until they came to a dam at a town called New Salem, where the flatboat got stuck and began to fill with water. It looked as though their voyage would end in disaster, until Abraham solved the problem. He and his partners unloaded part of the cargo to lighten the boat. Then Abraham drilled a hole in the bottom to let some of the water drain out. As the boat became lighter, it slid over the dam. Abraham then pegged the hole and they were on their way again.

From that point, Abraham and his partners made their way to New Orleans without any more adventures. In three months Abraham was back in New Salem. He was now twenty-two years old in a new place without any money. When he was offered a job as a clerk in Mr. Offutt's store, though, Abraham decided to stay.

In 1830, New Salem was a typical frontier town made up mostly of log cabins. Still, it was the largest place Abraham had ever lived in. It had two saloons, a tavern, and two general stores. Some of the cabins even had glass windows! There were a few educated folks in the town, including two doctors, the tavern owner, and the local schoolmaster. Most of the townspeople, though, were farmers like Abraham's father. For entertainment they had dances, held foot races and wrestling matches, or got into fights at the saloons.

As a new person in such a place, Abraham was anxious to prove that he was tough, so he competed in races, showed off his skill with an ax, and got into a number of fights. One of the people he impressed was Denton Offutt, his boss. Mr. Offutt boasted that Abraham, who was now 6 feet 4 inches (1.8 m) tall, was the best wrestler in town. This angered a man named Jack Armstrong. Mr. Armstrong was the leader of a local gang called the "Clary Grove Boys," and he considered himself to be the village wrestling champion.

To settle the dispute, a match was arranged between the two men. Mr. Offutt bet ten dollars that Abraham would throw Jack Armstrong. A large crowd showed up to watch the fight, which was held near the banks of the Sangamon River. After a long struggle, Abraham gained the advantage. When it looked as though he was about to win, the rest of the Clary gang jumped into the fight. This made Abraham angry. With his back to the river, he yelled that he was ready to take on each one of them. Strangely enough, it was Jack Armstrong who saved Abraham from what probably would have been an awful beating. Mr. Armstrong was so impressed with his opponent's courage that he shook Abraham's hand and declared the match a draw. From that point on, the "Clary Grove Boys" accepted Abraham Lincoln as their leader. He had shown that he was tough. The prominent people in town, however, considered him to be a ruffian.

Fortunately, Abraham did not keep this reputation for long. During the next few years, he earned a living doing a variety of jobs. At different times he was a storekeeper, the town postmaster, and a land surveyor. He did not make much money at any of these occupations, but he did become well known for his honesty.

One day, for example, a farmer's wife came into Mr. Offutt's store and bought 4 ounces (28 gr) of tea. After the woman left, Abraham noticed that she had forgotten half of her purchase. Even though she lived ten miles out of town, he walked out to her house that evening to bring her the remaining tea.

During these years, Abraham became interested in politics—the question of how the government should be run and what laws should be passed. As a young boy in Indiana, he had enjoyed listening to grown-ups argue about politics. In New Salem he voted in an election for the first time, and he frequently discussed political issues with the customers in Mr. Offutt's store.

People on the frontier cared about politics, because the government had a direct effect on their lives. For example, if the government decided not to construct a new road, many farmers would not be able to get their crops to market. If the government charged too high a price for land, many people would not be able to buy farms. Political issues like these mattered a great deal to people in New Salem.

In 1834 Abraham decided to try a career in politics. That year he ran for the state legislature, which had the job of passing laws for the people of Illinois. Abraham campaigned by traveling around the district (which included New Salem) and talking to the voters. In one place he went to work in the fields with a group of farmhands. When Abraham was able to harvest more wheat than any of them, the men were so impressed that they all decided to vote for him. Many more people supported him because of his reputation for honesty, and in August 1834, he was elected to the Illinois legislature. Abraham Lincoln had come a long way since his arrival in New Salem in 1830. The prominent people no longer thought he was a ruffian.

Several months later he traveled to Vandalia, the state capital, where the legislature met. Vandalia was a more impressive place than New Salem. It was larger, and some of its people lived in wooden frame houses rather than log cabins. Still, compared to cities like New Orleans, it was a primitive place. The streets were unpaved, and during the rainy season, mosquitos and flies invaded the town. People joked that the flies were big enough to kill a horse!

The statehouse, where the legislature met, was a brick building that was impressive-looking from the outside. The inside was another matter. The lawmakers sat at long tables in a large hall. On the floor were sandboxes into which the men could spit tobacco juice. It was not unusual for plaster to fall from the ceiling while somebody was giving a speech. The statehouse was slowly crumbling.

During his first year in the legislature, Abraham decided that he wanted to become a lawyer. In order to practice law, a person had to pass a test called a bar exam. Today, if a person wants to take this exam, she or he must attend law school. This was not necessary in the 1830s. In fact, there were very few law schools in the United States at that time. Abraham prepared for the exam by borrowing books from a friend who was a lawyer.

He spent as much of his free time as possible reading law. On nice days he could often be seen lying under a tree studying a law book or walking down a road reciting a legal case to himself. After about two years of study, Abraham took and passed the bar exam.

Abraham enjoyed being a member of the legislature. He was popular with the other lawmakers, and he worked hard to get the state government to build roads and canals for the farmers. In 1836, however, he and the other legislators were forced to deal with the troublesome issue of slavery.

By this time there were over 2,000,000 black slaves living on plantations in the South. They worked in the fields, growing the cotton, tobacco, sugar, and rice that made their owners wealthy. Yet slaves had absolutely no rights. They were simply property. In return for their labor, they received only ragged clothes and poor shelter and food. They were paid no wages. Slaves could be whipped for not working hard enough, and they could be sold like animals. Owners sometimes even broke up slave families by selling parents and children to different people.

Some slaves resisted this harsh treatment. In 1831 a slave named Nat Turner led an uprising in Virginia. Before this revolt was crushed, sixty whites and two hundred blacks were killed. From that time onward, plantation owners became very frightened that other slaves might rise up against their masters.

During the same time, some Northern whites and free blacks began to demand the abolition of slavery. These people became known as abolitionists, and they made speeches and wrote newspaper articles describing how terrible life was for the slaves. They also helped some slaves escape to Canada.

There were no slaves in Illinois, but there were abolitionists in the state. In 1836 some Southern whites wrote to the governor of Illinois and demanded that he stop the activities of these abolitionists. The Southerners felt that the abolitionists were troublemakers who were trying to start revolts like Nat Turner's. The Illinois governor sympathized with the Southerners and asked the legislature for its opinion. This is why Abraham Lincoln was forced to think about slavery again.

Abraham had mixed feelings about the problem. Like most whites, he was prejudiced against black people. He did not want blacks to vote, and he did not think they were as good as whites. Abraham also disagreed with the abolitionists. He felt that their harsh attacks on the plantation owners were causing Southern whites to distrust Northerners.

Yet Abraham was deeply troubled by slavery. He had studied American history and had come to believe that slavery went against important American ideals. Americans had rebelled against England, Abraham thought, because the English king had tried to take away their freedom. The Declaration of Independence had said that "all men are created equal" and that God has given them the rights of "life, liberty, and the pursuit of happiness." If these things were true, then how could one human being own another human being? As Abraham Lincoln thought about this question, he concluded that slavery must be wrong. Black people might not be his equals, he thought, but they had the right to be free.

When the governor of Illinois asked the legislature to support the plantation owners against the abolitionists, Abraham voted "no." He did not like the abolitionists, but he would not support slavery. Only five other lawmakers agreed with him. The other seventy-seven sided with the slaveowners. Abraham Lincoln had taken his first public stand against slavery.

COURTSHIP
AND MARRIAGE

—4—

In late 1836 the legislature recessed and Abraham returned home to New Salem. He was now twenty-seven, an age when most men were married. Because he was so shy around women, though, Abraham was still a bachelor. He probably remembered how girls had teased him when he was a boy, and he still believed that women thought he was ugly.

That fall, though, he met a woman named Mary Owen. For a while, the two courted, but their romance did not go well. As she got to know him, Mary decided that Abraham was ungentlemanly. He did not treat her the way a man was expected to treat a woman. One day they went horseback riding with some friends. When the group came to a stream, the other men helped their women friends across. Abraham did not. He just rode through the stream and expected Mary to follow.

Mary also felt that Abraham was not romantic enough. He called her "my friend," and he never said anything tender to her. After a year, Mary finally decided that he did not really care about her, so she stopped seeing him.

Abraham was shocked by this rejection. Once again he decided that women did not like him. "I have now come to the conclusion," he wrote to a friend, "never again to think of marrying; and for this reason, I can never be satisfied with any one who would be block-head enough to have me."

In 1837 Abraham moved again, this time to Springfield, Illinois, which had replaced Vandalia as the state capital. Springfield was a larger and more impressive town than the old capital. It had about 2,000 people, some beautiful large houses, several schools, and six churches. It even had some stores where a person could buy luxury goods like silk, fancy boots, and china dishes.

But Abraham noticed that in many ways Springfield was still a frontier town. Like Vandalia, it had unpaved streets where pigs rooted for food. During the rainy season, the streets became huge pools of mud that were almost impossible to cross.

Abraham had no trouble finding a place to live in Springfield. Shortly after he arrived, he met a store owner named Joshua Speed. Joshua liked Abraham and offered to share his room above the store with the newcomer. Abraham accepted. The two men became close friends. Because Joshua's room did not have a kitchen, Abraham ate his meals at the home of another friend.

During his first few years in Springfield, Abraham worked hard at being a lawyer and a member of the state legislature. He did not think about finding a wife. Then in December 1839, he met a woman named Mary Todd at a dance.

Mary Todd and Abraham Lincoln were as unlikely a couple as a person could imagine. About the only thing they had in common was that both of their families came from Kentucky. They didn't even look like they belonged together. He was 6 feet 4 inches (1.8 m) tall, thin, and not at all handsome. She was 5 feet 2 inches (1.5 m) tall, a bit plump, and rather pretty. He came from a poor pioneer family. Her father was a wealthy banker who owned a plantation and many slaves.

Abraham had been convinced that he would never marry. Mary had come to live with her sister in Springfield in order to find a husband. Even their personalities were very different. He was shy and calm on the outside. She liked to flirt with men and had a very bad temper.

In spite of these differences, or maybe because of them, Abraham Lincoln and Mary Todd liked each other from the very beginning. She liked his sense of humor. He enjoyed her liveliness. They both were interested in politics. After meeting Mary at the dance, Abraham wanted to see her again.

But he could not simply visit her whenever he pleased. Mary was living with her sister and brother-in-law, Elizabeth and Ninian Edwards. They were looking after her while she was in Springfield, and they had to approve of any man she saw. So, according to the customs of that time, the Edwardses had to give their approval before Abraham could visit Mary. Fortunately, Joshua Speed knew Elizabeth and Ninian Edwards and arranged for his friend, Abraham Lincoln, to call upon Mary Todd.

Abraham and Mary soon fell in love and courted for about a year. In December 1840 they became engaged to be married, but the Edwardses found out and became furious. They had been willing to allow Mary to see Abraham, but marriage to him was out of the question. In their eyes, his lower-class background made him an unsuitable husband for Mary. Mary didn't agree, but that didn't matter. Abraham Lincoln was no longer permitted to visit her, and their engagement was broken off.

For over a year Mary Todd and Abraham Lincoln stayed apart. But they still thought about each other. Finally, in the summer of 1842, a friend named Mrs. Francis arranged for them to meet at her house. In this way, Mary and Abraham got back together. For months afterward, they met secretly at the Francis home, and in the fall they decided to get married.

Mary's sister and brother-in-law did not find out about the marriage plans until the morning of the wedding. The Edwardses still did not like Abraham, but when they realized that Mary was determined to marry him, they gave their approval. They also offered to have the wedding in their home.

On a stormy November evening in 1842, Abraham Lincoln and Mary Todd were married in the parlor of the Edwardses' mansion. He was thirty-three and she was twenty-three. Abraham gave Mary a ring with the words "Love is eternal" engraved on it. A small number of friends witnessed the ceremony, but none of Abraham's relatives was invited. They reminded him of his poor background, which the Edwardses had disliked. Abraham did not even tell his parents about his wedding until much later, and he never took Mary to meet them.

After the ceremony, the Lincolns moved into a room that they rented at the Globe Tavern in Springfield. Abraham could not yet afford to buy a house, and rent and food at the tavern cost only four dollars a week. Life at the Globe was not easy for the young couple. Mary was accustomed to great luxury and had a hard time adjusting to living in a single room. Because there was so little space, she was not even able to entertain her friends. Things became even more crowded after the birth of their first son, Robert.

Abraham, too, was ashamed of living in the tavern, so he worked hard and saved his money. In about a year, the Lincolns were able to buy a house with a nice yard. By the time their second son, Edward, was born in 1846, Abraham was making enough money to hire a maid to help Mary clean the house and care for the children.

That same year Abraham was elected to the United States Congress, which made laws for the entire country. This meant that the Lincolns had to move from Springfield to the nation's capital, Washington, D.C. The trip to Washington showed how much the United States had changed since Abraham Lincoln's childhood. When his family had moved from Kentucky to Indiana in 1816, they had gone on foot and had cut their own path through the wilderness. Now there were railroads that carried people over long distances.

Washington had been planned as the nation's capital many years before Abraham's birth, but when he and his family arrived there in 1847, it was still unfinished. Abraham saw a city in which great mansions stood next to small shacks. He noticed that there were still cowsheds in the backyards of many homes. He watched people dump garbage into the unpaved streets where it was eaten by wandering geese, chickens, and pigs. He even discovered that the White House, where the president lived, was located near a swamp that was a breeding place for mosquitos in the summer.

None of this surprised Abraham. After all, he had grown up on the frontier, where conditions were even rougher. There was one thing about Washington, though, that shocked him. There was a slave market near the Capitol building. Slavery was bad enough, he thought, but it was an absolute disgrace that human beings were bought and sold in the nation's capital.

While Abraham was in Congress, the Lincolns lived in a boarding house. Mary was uncomfortable there because it reminded her of the days when they had lived at the Globe Tavern. Once again, she could not entertain people, and as a result, the Lincolns were rarely invited to other people's homes. Mary soon became bored with this life, and, after a few months, she took Robert and Eddie to Kentucky to visit her father. Abraham was lonely without his family, but he filled his time by working.

When Abraham's term in Congress ended in 1849, he did not run for reelection. Instead, he returned home to Springfield to be with his family and to practice law. In the next few years, there were many changes in the Lincoln family.

A few months after Abraham had come back from Washington, his younger son, Eddie, became seriously ill. For over a month Abraham and Mary cared for the sick boy, but he did not get better. On the morning of February 1, 1850, Eddie Lincoln died. He was only four years old. The Lincolns were almost crushed by his death. For weeks Mary stayed in her room and cried. Only Abraham was able to get her to eat anything.

Fortunately, after Eddie's death, happier times returned to the Lincoln family. Over the next few months the Lincolns slowly recovered from their grief, and at the end of the year, Mary gave birth to another son, who was named Willie. The Lincolns were delighted with their new child. Then, in 1853, Mary gave birth to another boy who was called Tad, because he wiggled around like a tadpole. The Lincolns now had three sons. Abraham loved his children and enjoyed playing with them. When Willie and Tad were young, he liked to lie on the living room floor, toss them into the air, and catch them. As the boys grew older, he encouraged them to be curious and to ask questions. Although it was common at this time for parents to beat disobedient children, Abraham Lincoln never hit his sons.

Abraham had settled into a quiet life in Springfield. He had come a long way since his pioneer beginnings in Kentucky. He was now a successful lawyer, happily married, and the father of three boys.

"A HOUSE DIVIDED
AGAINST ITSELF"

5

While Abraham Lincoln was raising a family and practicing law in Springfield, the nation was becoming more and more divided over slavery. The abolitionists had persuaded many Northerners that slavery was a great moral evil. Furthermore, the United States had recently conquered a great deal of land in the West as a result of a war with Mexico. Northern whites did not want slavery to spread into the new territories. Northern farmers, for example, worried that Southern plantation owners would get all of the best new land. By the 1850s, a majority of Northerners agreed that slavery should not be allowed in the new territories.

Southern slaveowners, on the other hand, felt differently. They wanted to be able to bring slaves into the West. The plantation owners defended slavery as a good thing for black people. The planters said that blacks were incapable of looking after themselves. At least when they were slaves, said the planters, blacks would be cared for.

During this time Abraham Lincoln was doing a lot of thinking about the question of slavery, and he was more convinced than ever that it was wrong. "If the Negro is a man," he said, "why my ancient faith teaches me that 'all men are created equal'; and that there can be no moral right in connection with one man's making a slave of another." He felt that slavery was wrong because it deprived black people of the right to be paid for the work they did. Abraham had noticed that many Southerners had said that slavery was a "very good thing," but he had never heard of any free man who was willing to be "a slave himself."

Many people agreed that slavery was bad, but they wondered how it should be ended. Abraham realized that this was a difficult question. He felt that the United States Constitution did not give the government the power to outlaw slavery where it already existed. As a result, he thought that slavery could not be made illegal in the southern states. But he did believe that the government could prevent slavery from spreading into the new territories. In fact, this is what he thought the government should do.

Abraham also hoped that Southerners could be shown that slavery was a bad system. If this happened, he thought, the plantation owners might be persuaded to free their slaves voluntarily. Still, Abraham was influenced by prejudice against blacks. He did not believe that whites and freed blacks would be able to live together as equals in the United States. Abraham and many other whites thought that because the ancestors of the slaves had come from Africa, the slaves should be sent back there after they were freed. However, very few blacks wanted to return to Africa. After all, America was their home, too!

Most members of Congress did not agree with Abraham's views about slavery. In 1854 Congress passed a law

CAUTION!!

COLORED PEOPLE

OF BOSTON, ONE & ALL,

You are hereby respectfully CAUTIONED and advised, to avoid conversing with the

Watchmen and Police Officers of Boston,

For since the recent ORDER OF THE MAYOR & ALDERMEN, they are empowered to act as

KIDNAPPERS
AND
Slave Catchers,

And they have already been actually employed in KIDNAPPING, CATCHING, AND KEEPING SLAVES. Therefore, if you value your LIBERTY, and the *Welfare of the Fugitives* among you, *Shun* them in every possible manner, as so many *HOUNDS* on the track of the most unfortunate of your race.

Keep a Sharp Look Out for KIDNAPPERS, and have TOP EYE open.

APRIL 24, 1851.

A handbill warning the black people of Boston to beware of the enforcement of fugitive slave laws that allowed slavery in two territories where it had once been illegal. These territories were Kansas and Nebraska; the law was called the Kansas-Nebraska Act. The Kansas-Nebraska Act said that the white people of each territory could decide for themselves whether they wanted slavery.

Almost immediately, southerners poured into Kansas with their slaves. In order to prevent the Southerners from getting control of Kansas, many northern antislavery farmers also moved into the territory. Soon a small war broke out in Kansas between the proslavery and antislavery settlers. Many people were killed.

The war in Kansas made antislavery Northerners furious. Violence had occurred because the government had allowed slavery to spread. These people were so angry that they got together and formed a new political party called the Republican party. The supporters of the new party hoped to stop the spread of slavery by electing a Republican president and a Republican Congress. Abraham Lincoln liked this idea, so he joined the new party in 1856. When he wasn't busy with his family or his law practice, he spent a great deal of time making antislavery speeches and helping Republicans get elected to office.

Abraham worked so hard for the Republicans that in 1858 they chose him to be their candidate for United States senator from Illinois. His opponent in the election was Senator Stephen A. Douglas, the man who had proposed the hated Kansas-Nebraska Act. Senator Douglas had a big advantage in this contest because he was much more famous than Abraham.

At the beginning of the campaign, Abraham made an important speech. The United States was like a house, he said, and

A house divided against itself cannot stand. I believe that this government cannot endure permanently half slave and half free. I do not expect the Union [the country] to be dissolved—I do not expect the house to fall—but I do expect it will cease to be divided. It will become all one thing or the other.

Abraham was afraid that if the slavery question was not settled soon, the country would fall apart. He believed that the Southerners wanted slavery to be legal everywhere in the United States. He and the Republicans wanted to see it come to an end everywhere in the United States. Many people in Illinois agreed with what Abraham Lincoln said in this speech.

Senator Douglas had very different views about slavery. The United States government, he said, "was made by the white man, for the benefit of the white man." If whites in one state wanted to have slavery, the Senator said, then they should be allowed to have it. He did not care what black people wanted. He told his supporters that Abraham was wrong. "This government," he said, "can endure forever, divided into free and slave States as our fathers made it."

Senator Douglas did not like black people, and he knew that many whites felt the same way. He told the voters of Illinois that if Abraham Lincoln and the Republicans got their way, all of the slaves would be freed and would come to Illinois to take land and jobs from white people.

Abraham fought hard to win the election. He traveled all over the state explaining his ideas about slavery to the voters. The election was close, but in the end Senator Douglas won. Many of the white people had believed that Senator Douglas was right when he had warned that blacks would take over the state if slavery were ended.

Even though Abraham Lincoln lost the election, he gained something very important. Newspapers from all over the country had reported his speeches. Many Northerners agreed with his attacks on slavery. As a result of the election, he had become an important leader of the Republican party.

The Republicans chose Abraham to be their candidate for president of the United States in 1860. Slavery was the most important issue in this election. Abraham Lincoln and the Republicans said that they would outlaw slavery in the new territories, but they would not try to abolish it in the South, because the Constitution protected it there.

The Southerners did not believe Abraham. They were convinced that if he won, he would immediately free all the slaves. The Southerners believed that only a president from the South could prevent this from happening. When the Democratic party nominated Stephen A. Douglas, the Southerners chose their own candidate for president, John C. Breckenridge of Kentucky. A fourth man, John Bell, also ran against Abraham.

Because there were four candidates, nobody won a majority of the votes. Abraham Lincoln got more votes than any of his opponents, so he was elected president of the United States. Not long after the election, a young girl wrote to him and said that he would look better with a beard. Abraham liked this suggestion and started to grow a beard. This was only the first of many changes that being president would bring to his life.

HARD CHOICES

—6—

The day after he was elected president, Abraham Lincoln said to a group of newspaper reporters, "Well, boys, your troubles are over now, mine have just begun." He meant that he was now responsible for running the government of the entire United States. He could not guess how much of a burden that responsibility would become.

Abraham's troubles, and the nation's, soon began. His election had angered southern leaders. Even though Abraham had said many times that he only wanted to stop the *spread* of slavery, these Southerners believed that he would free all of the slaves after he became president.

Some of the southern leaders became convinced that the only way to prevent this was to secede from the Union, just as the American colonies had broken away from England in 1776. These people argued that the South had to become an independent nation if it was going to prevent northern interference in slavery.

Mary Todd Lincoln and sons

In December 1860 South Carolina became the first southern state to leave the Union. By February, Mississippi, Florida, Alabama, Georgia, Louisiana, and Texas had also seceded. Representatives of these seven states then gathered in Montgomery, Alabama, and created a new nation called the Confederate States of America. They elected a man named Jefferson Davis to be their president, and they wrote a constitution that guaranteed white people the right to own black slaves.

Abraham was terribly upset by this news. He had not yet been sworn in as president, and the country was beginning to fall apart. Still, there was nothing he could do about it until his inauguration (when he took the oath of office), and this would not happen until March 1861.

As the inauguration approached, many of Abraham's friends believed that Southerners would try to kill him. By the time Abraham was ready to leave for the capital, he was worried, too. On his last day in Springfield, Abraham told his law partner, "If I live, I'm coming back some time, and then we'll go right on practicing law as if nothing had ever happened." When Abraham left his law office that day, he was no longer sure that he would ever return.

The next morning, Abraham Lincoln and his family boarded a train for Washington, D.C. On that dark, rainy February day, 1,000 people gathered at the station to say goodbye. As the drizzle fell, Lincoln stood at the rear of the train and thanked the people of Springfield for their friendship. "My friends," he told them,

> No one, not in my situation, can appreciate my feeling of sadness at this parting. To this place, and the kindness of these people, I owe every thing.

Here I have lived a quarter of a century [twenty-five years], and have passed from a young to an old man. Here my children have been born, and one is buried. I now leave, not knowing when, or whether ever, I may return.

Because the train stopped in many towns, it was a long ride to Washington. People all over the North wanted to see the new president. The most dangerous stop on the route was Baltimore, Maryland. The railroad line did not run straight through Baltimore, so Abraham and his family would have to get off the train at one station and ride by carriage to another station at the opposite end of the city. Then they would board a second train that would take them the rest of the way to Washington.

There were many Confederate sympathizers in Baltimore who might try to shoot Lincoln as he traveled through the streets to the second railway station. In order to prevent this, his friends came up with a secret plan. Lincoln would travel between stations in disguise at night and he would be guarded by his friend, Ward Lamon Hill, who was armed with four guns and two knives.

Abraham arrived in Baltimore on February 22, 1861, and that evening was transported to the second train, which left for Washington immediately. It was an uncomfortable night for him. His sleeping compartment was too short, and he was embarrassed that he had been forced to sneak into Washington. But the plan worked. On February 23, Abraham arrived safely in the capital.

Soon afterward, on March 4, Abraham was inaugurated as the sixteenth president of the United States. The weather was dreary that day, and troops were stationed throughout

*The inauguration of Lincoln
in front of the Capitol*

the city to protect the new president. Despite this, thousands of people gathered outside the capital to hear his inauguration speech.

Standing under cloudy skies, Abraham declared that secession was illegal, and that it was his duty to preserve the union. But he also tried to reassure the Southerners that he meant them no harm. He promised that he would not abolish slavery in the South. He also said that he would not use the army against the Confederate states unless they attacked the United States government first.

Then, President Lincoln told the Southerners that they could end the crisis. "In *your* hands my dissatisfied fellow countrymen," he said,

> and not mine, is the momentous [important] issue of civil war. The government will not assail [attack] you. You have no conflict without yourselves being the aggressors. You have no oath registered in heaven to destroy the government, while I shall have the most solemn one to "preserve, protect and defend" it.

At the end of his speech, the president said, "I am loath [reluctant] to close. We are not enemies but friends. We must not be enemies." The president hoped that the Southerners would come to their senses and rejoin the Union without war.

Lincoln was stunned the next day when he received a message that Confederate soldiers had surrounded Fort Sumter, in Charleston, South Carolina. Fort Sumter was located on an island in the middle of Charleston harbor, and it belonged to the United States government. Major

Robert Anderson, the commander of the fort, told the president that his men were outnumbered and would soon have to surrender if they were not reinforced.

Abraham Lincoln now faced the hardest choice of his career. Should he send help to Fort Sumter? He had promised not to use force against the Confederates unless they started fighting first. The Southerners had surrounded the fort, but they had not yet fired at it. If President Lincoln did not send help, Major Anderson and his men would soon run out of food. But if he did reinforce the fort, the Confederates might start shooting. This would mean war. President Lincoln did not want to be responsible for the beginning of bloodshed.

The president could not decide what to do. He asked his advisors for help, but they could not agree on a plan. Finally, after thinking about the problem for three weeks, President Lincoln decided to send reinforcements to Fort Sumter. If the Confederates attacked, he thought, they would be responsible for starting a war.

The president wondered anxiously what would happen. One night he had a strange dream. In the dream he was on a ghost ship that was sailing quickly toward a shore that he could barely see. As wind blew the ship across the water, Abraham wondered what he would find when he got to that shore. When he woke up, Abraham was puzzled by the dream. It seemed to be a warning that he was moving toward some danger, but he did not completely understand what it meant.

Then, a few days later, the president received a message that the Confederates had begun to bombard Fort Sumter before the reinforcements had arrived. Major Anderson and his men were not able to hold out for long,

The bombardment of Fort Sumter,
the beginning of the Civil War

and on April 13, 1861, they surrendered. War had begun! But this was not a war of one nation against another nation. It was a civil war—a struggle between people of the same country.

President Lincoln reacted quickly to the news of Fort Sumter's fall. The Confederate states had now rebelled against the United States government. The president immediately called for 75,000 volunteers to join the army and put down the rebellion. Throughout the North, people rallied to defend the Union. In one town, a judge and jury left a courtroom together to join the army. The governor of Iowa begged the president to send him guns, because men in his state were volunteering faster than they could be armed.

President Lincoln's proclamation made Southerners angry. Thousands of them joined the Confederate army. On top of that, Virginia, which was just across the Potomac River from Washington, seceded. Soon afterward, three more southern states (Arkansas, North Carolina, and Tennessee) joined the Confederacy. Four other slave states (Maryland, Missouri, Kentucky, and Delaware) stayed in the Union, but it looked as though they might secede at any moment.

The president faced some difficult problems at the beginning of the war. He had to keep the remaining four slave states from joining the Confederacy, and he had to defend a capital that was almost surrounded by enemies. There were very few soldiers in Washington, and reinforcements had to pass through Maryland, which was filled with Confederate sympathizers. In fact, about a week after the war began, Union soldiers on their way to Washington were attacked in the streets of Baltimore, Maryland.

For a while it looked as though the rebels would capture the capital. At night President Lincoln could see the Confederate campfires across the Potomac River in Virginia. Soon, though, reinforcements began to arrive in Washington. By the end of April, there were 10,000 soldiers in the city, with more arriving each day. President Lincoln could finally begin to think about attacking the Confederacy.

In these early days, before much fighting had occurred, people on both sides had very unrealistic ideas about war. President Lincoln had never been in a battle, and neither had most other Americans. When the president had called for volunteers, he had asked them to serve in the army for only three months. He thought that the war would last only that long.

Most people in the North and the South agreed with him. Each side believed that it had the bravest men and would easily defeat the enemy. To the young men in both armies, war at first seemed like an exciting adventure. They got to wear colorful uniforms and march in parades while people cheered and bands played stirring music.

Most of these young men did not think much about killing or being killed. They thought that battle would be like a big game. The soldiers in each army thought that they would charge, the enemy would retreat, and the war would be over. They soon learned how wrong these ideas were.

The first big battle of the Civil War occurred on July 21, 1861, when a Union army tried to attack the Confederate railroad center at Manassas, Virginia. The Northerners were so confident they would win a quick victory that many members of Congress and their wives rode out in their carriages to watch the battle. Some of these people even brought picnic lunches with them!

President Lincoln did not join the picnickers. He remained in Washington near the telegraph, where he anxiously awaited news of the struggle. It was a hot, humid day, and reports about the action were confusing. In the morning, the Union soldiers collided with the Confederate army near a stream called Bull Run in Virginia. The first messages to the president said that the Northerners were winning. Then came news that they were retreating. Another message said they were attacking again.

By the end of the day, the president learned the truth. The Union army had been defeated and had been driven from the battlefield. In the evening, President Lincoln saw Union soldiers streaming back into Washington, bringing several thousand wounded men with them. They had left about five hundred of their comrades dead on the battlefield.

Now President Lincoln realized the awful truth. The war would not end quickly. It would be long, terrible, and bloody.

THE LONG STRUGGLE

7

The new year began with tragedy for the Lincoln family. In February 1862 both Willie and Tad became ill. Tad recovered, but Willie got worse. For many days Abraham and Mary took turns bathing his face with a wet cloth to keep his fever down. It did no good. At five o'clock in the afternoon of February 20, Willie Lincoln died. Abraham looked down at his dead son and whispered, "My poor boy, he was too good for this earth. . . ." Then he left the room and burst into tears.

After Willie's death, Abraham paid even greater attention to Tad. Although he was busy running the government and managing a great war, President Lincoln kept his office door open for his youngest son. Sometimes Tad came in and fell asleep on the office couch while his father was busy working. When this happened, Abraham took Tad to his bedroom, rocked him, and then put him to bed. When

The president and son Tad

Abraham had free time, he often took Tad horseback riding. Still, the president could not forget his dead son. At times he dreamt that Willie was alive and playing on the White House lawn.

News from the battlefront was also bad. In the spring, a huge Northern army of over 100,000 men launched an attack on the Confederate capital of Richmond. The Southerners were outnumbered, but they had better generals. They defeated the Union army and drove it from Richmond.

To make matters worse, President Lincoln got into a fight with his own party over slavery. At the beginning of the war, many of the Republicans urged the president to emancipate (free) the slaves. These Republicans reminded him that slavery was a great evil and that it had caused the war that was now tearing apart the Union.

President Lincoln faced another difficult choice. He, too, thought that slavery was wrong. He, too, wanted the slaves to be free. But he knew that many Northern whites hated black people. He believed that these whites would not be willing to fight a war to free the slaves. Mr. Lincoln was also afraid that if he abolished slavery, the remaining southern states (Maryland, Kentucky, Delaware, and Missouri) would join the Confederacy. He was convinced that if the Union side became divided, it would lose the war.

President Lincoln decided not to free the slaves in early 1862. He said to the Republicans, "My paramount [main] object is to save the Union, and is *not* either to save or destroy slavery."

But Abraham Lincoln's wife, Mary, also thought the slaves should be freed. Even though she had grown up on a plantation, in the White House Mary Lincoln had become best friends with a former slave named Elizabeth Keckley.

Mrs. Keckley, who was the White House dressmaker, had comforted Mary after Willie's death.

Mrs. Keckley made Mary realize how awful it was to be a slave. She described being beaten by her former owner. She told Mary about seeing a boy sold away from his mother so that the plantation owner could get money to pay for some pigs. After hearing these stories, Mary became a strong opponent of slavery. By 1862 she was helping to take care of runaway slaves who had come to Washington, D.C.

Perhaps Mary influenced her husband, because by the summer of 1862, President Lincoln had changed his mind

come convinced that free-

ıg to do and that it would

ident believed that if the

would have to leave the

e farms and plantations of

to issue an Emancipation

ern victory. Unfortunately,

Inion armies were doing

the Confederates, under

the North. On the foggy

northern army caught up

called Antietam Creek in

that raged for the entire

back to Virginia.

ictory as a sign from God

e the slaves. On January 1,

ed the Emancipation Proclamation. not completely end slavery. It freed nfederacy but not those in the southern

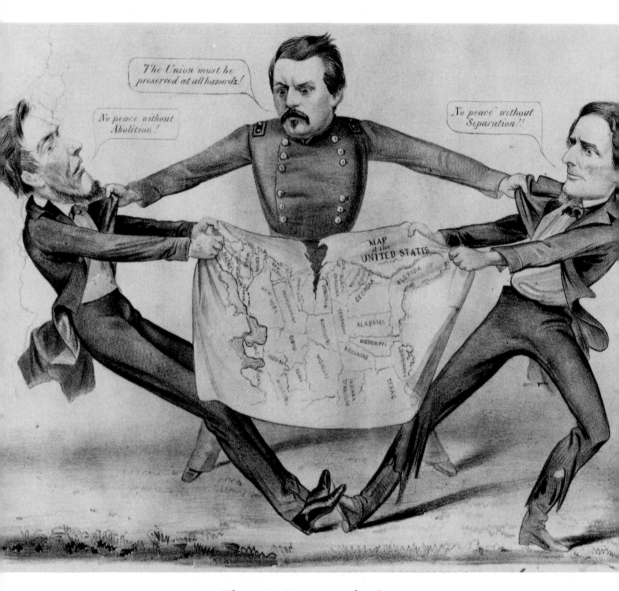

The War Between the States
split the nation.

The Emancipation Proclamation

states that had remained loyal to the Union. President Lincoln was still afraid that these states might secede.

The Emancipation Proclamation was the beginning of the end of slavery in the United States. After it was issued, many slaves ran away from their owners. Thousands of these freed slaves later joined the Union army.

In 1863 the tide began to turn against the South. That summer the Confederates invaded the North again. When the Union army moved to stop them, there was another great battle, this time at a place called Gettysburg in Pennsylvania. The fighting at Gettysburg lasted three days. On the third day, General Lee sent his best soldiers across an open field under the hot summer sun to attack the Union army. At first it looked as though nothing could stop the Confederates. They briefly raised their flag at the center of the Union line, but then they were driven back. The Confederates had been defeated, and they were forced to retreat.

The Battle of Gettysburg was the most terrible battle of the Civil War. Ten thousand men died there. Afterward, some people decided to build a special cemetery for the dead soldiers. President Lincoln was invited to give a speech at the opening of the cemetery.

When the president arrived in Gettysburg on November 18, 1863, he could see bullet holes in houses, and trees damaged in the battle. The next day he rode out to the cemetery and spoke to a huge crowd.

He told his audience that the war was more than just a struggle to defeat the Confederacy. It was also a fight to guarantee freedom and equality to all Americans. "Fourscore and seven [eighty-seven] years ago," he said,

*The first reading of the Emancipation
Proclamation before the Cabinet*

Lincoln at Antietam, Maryland, during the Civil War. On Lincoln's right is Allan Pinkerton, detective and first chief of the Secret Service; on his left, Major General John A. McClernand.

our fathers brought forth on this continent, a new nation, conceived in liberty and dedicated to the proposition that all men are created equal. Now we are engaged in a great civil war, testing whether that nation, or any other nation so conceived and so dedicated can long endure.

At the end of his speech, President Lincoln asked the American people to continue the struggle. That way they could make sure that the Union soldiers at Gettysburg "shall not have died in vain [uselessly]; that this nation, under God, shall have a new birth of freedom; and that the government of the people, by the people, for the people, shall not perish from the earth."

When the president was finished, the audience cheered and applauded wildly. President Lincoln's Gettysburg Address became so famous that for a hundred years afterward, American schoolchildren learned it by heart.

In the spring of 1864, the Union army launched another attack on Richmond. President Lincoln believed that this might be the last year of the war. The commander of the Union forces, a man named Ulysses S. Grant, was a great general. He had a huge army of 120,000 men and a good plan for defeating the Confederacy.

The Confederate army was much smaller than the Union army, but its commander, Robert E. Lee, was as good a general as Ulysses S. Grant. When the Union troops moved toward Richmond, they became tangled up in a heavy forest. The Confederates attacked, and for almost a month the two armies fought a series of bloody battles in the Virginia wilderness. In the end, General Grant did not capture Richmond, and 60,000 of his men had been killed or wounded.

Giving the Gettysburg Address

Executive Mansion
Washington, Nov 21, 1864

To Mrs Bixby, Boston, Mass,
    Dear Madam,

      I have been shown in the files of the War Department a statement of the Adjutant General of Massachusetts that you are the mother of five sons who have died gloriously on the field of battle I feel how weak and fruitless must be any word of mine which should attempt to beguile you from the grief of a loss so overwhelming. But I cannot refrain from tendering you the consolation that may be found in the thanks of the republic they died to save I pray that our Heavenly Father may assuage the anguish of your bereavement, and leave you only the cherished memory of the loved and lost, and the solemn pride that must be yours to have laid so costly a sacrifice upon the altar of freedom

    Yours very sincerely and respectfully.

      A. Lincoln.

*A letter from President Lincoln to a woman
who lost five sons in the Civil War*

Northerners were horrified by the bloodshed. Never had American armies suffered such terrible losses in battle. Even one of the president's advisors wrote, "The immense slaughter of our brave men chills and sickens us all." Day after day ambulances carried the dead and wounded back to Washington.

Some people in the North were so angry that they began to protest against the war. They could see no purpose in all the killing. Some of them demanded that President Lincoln fire General Grant. Other people urged the president to make peace and grant the Confederacy its independence. The president faced more hard choices. Should he fire General Grant? Should he end the war?

Abraham Lincoln refused to make peace with the South. The Confederate armies had also suffered terrible losses, and they had fewer men to replace the ones who had been killed and wounded. And the president still believed that it was worth fighting a war to preserve the Union and to free the slaves.

President Lincoln had now decided to take the final step towards ending slavery. The Emancipation Proclamation had not freed the slaves in the southern states that had remained in the Union. In the summer of 1864, Lincoln called for an amendment to the Constitution that would make slavery illegal everywhere in the United States.

When the president's Northern opponents heard about this amendment, they were furious. They demanded that he stop trying to free the slaves, and when he refused to do this, they decided to try to replace him. There would be an election in November 1864, and during the summer it looked as though the president would be defeated.

Abraham Lincoln himself was convinced that he would lose. He was so unpopular that some people wanted to see

Lincoln visiting an army camp. Because so many battles were fought close to Washington, the president visited the men often.

him dead. One northern newspaper editor wrote, "If he is elected to misgovern for another four years, we trust some bold hand will pierce his heart with dagger point for the public good."

Then, suddenly, when things looked bleakest for the president, the Union forces won several great victories. In July they stopped the last Confederate invasion of the North, and in early September they captured the important southern city of Atlanta.

It was clear now that the war could not last much longer. The Union armies had conquered much of the Confederacy. One by one, the Southern armies were being defeated. The Confederates could no longer replace their dead soldiers. Even General Lee could not defend Richmond for much longer. Northerners realized all of this, and in November 1864 they reelected President Lincoln to a second term.

Abraham was happy that the country had chosen him as its leader again. On the evening of his second inauguration, he and Mary held a party. One of the people who wanted to congratulate the president was Frederick Douglass, a famous abolitionist. But because Mr. Douglass was a black man, the guards would not let him in to see President Lincoln. The war had not ended racial prejudice.

Frederick Douglass told the guards that he had as much right to visit the president as any other American. Lincoln overheard the argument and ordered the soldiers to let Mr. Douglass into the White House. The president shook Mr. Douglass's hand and said, "I am glad to see you."

The war had changed Abraham Lincoln. He had once believed that freed slaves should be sent back to Africa. Now he had become the first president to entertain a black person in the White House.

VICTORY AND DEATH

8

The war had changed Abraham Lincoln in another way. It had ruined his health. The president knew that he was not well. "The war is eating my life out," he said to a friend, "I shall not live to see the end." By the middle of March 1865, he was so sick that he actually held a meeting with his advisors in his bedroom.

The president's friends were more concerned about rumors that the Southerners might try to murder him. Lincoln tried not to worry about these threats. He said to his friend, Noah Brooks, "I long ago made up my mind that if anybody wants to kill me, he will do it. If I wore a shirt of mail [suit of armor] and kept myself surrounded by a bodyguard it would be all the same. There are a thousand ways of getting at a man if it is desired that he should be killed."

His friends and advisors did not believe this. They did everything they could to protect him. Secretary of War Edwin Stanton assigned four Washington policemen to guard the president and ordered a company of soldiers to camp on the White House lawn.

In spite of his poor health and the threats against his life, Lincoln decided to visit General Grant and the Union army at the end of March 1865. The general had told President Lincoln that the Northern forces were about to capture Richmond, and the president wanted to see the victory for himself.

On April 2 General Grant launched the final assault on the Confederate capital. That morning, hundreds of cannons bombarded the Confederate trenches. Then the Union soldiers charged. General Lee's men fought bravely, but they could not hold back the much larger Union army. The next day the Confederates retreated and the Northern soldiers marched into Richmond.

President Lincoln was still not well, but he wanted to visit the captured Confederate capital. He took Tad with him. When they arrived in Richmond, the city was in ruins. Many of the soldiers who accompanied the president were former slaves who had won their freedom in the war. When the white people of Richmond saw this, they were furious. Here is the man who ruined our way of life, they thought, and now he is allowing our slaves to control our city. Most of the whites stayed indoors that day.

The black people of Richmond felt differently. They poured into the streets to greet the president. One black woman said, "God bless you" to the president as he went by.

At the end of his walk, Abraham came to the abandoned home of Jefferson Davis, the Confederate president. When the president went inside and sat in Mr. Davis's chair, the Union soldiers cheered. Surely the end of the war was

Lincoln entering Richmond

very near. As President Lincoln sat in Jefferson Davis's home, though, he did not feel like celebrating. He was very tired, and he was saddened by all of the death and destruction that he had seen.

The president's gloomy mood did not end when he left Richmond. One night soon afterward, he had a strange dream. In the dream, he heard people crying while he was asleep in the White House. He got up to investigate, but he could not find out who was crying. Then he entered the East Room of the White House, where he saw a dead body lying on a platform. Around the platform were soldiers who were guarding the body. Nearby, he saw a crowd of people who were mourning for the dead person. When Abraham asked about the dead person, one of the soldiers said that it was the president who had been murdered. Then Abraham woke up. The dream had frightened him. What did it mean? After thinking about it, Abraham decided that he was not the dead man on the platform. The assassin (murderer) in the dream must have shot somebody else by mistake.

When President Lincoln returned to Washington on April 9, he heard glorious news. The Confederate army had been surrounded at a place called Appomattox Courthouse and had surrendered to General Grant. The war had finally ended. President Lincoln and Secretary of War Stanton were so happy that they hugged each other. The next day there were celebrations throughout Washington.

The end of the war lifted the president's spirits. On Friday, April 14, 1865, Lincoln awoke after his first good night's sleep in a long time. He had dreamt again, but this time it was the old dream in which he was on a ghost ship heading for a strange shore. The dream didn't frighten

Abraham, because he thought it was a sign that he would soon hear good news.

April 14 was a beautiful spring day. The air was sweet with the smell of blooming flowers. That morning Abraham and Mary ate breakfast together and discussed their plan to see a play that evening at Ford's Theater.

After breakfast, Abraham spent a full day working; then in the late afternoon, he went for a carriage ride with Mary. They talked about the future. After he was finished being president, Abraham wanted to travel. He wanted to visit Europe and the Holy Land. Then he would go back to practicing law.

When the Lincolns returned home for dinner, one of the president's bodyguards, George Crook, tried to persuade them not to go to the play. Detective Crook was worried because the newspapers had written about the Lincolns' theater plans. The detective thought that it would be very easy for somebody to kill the president at the play. Abraham was not worried and brushed off the detective's warning.

The president was not as safe as he had believed. By an incredible mistake, a policeman named John Parker was assigned to guard the Lincolns that evening. Officer Parker was a very unreliable man who had gotten into trouble several times for being drunk on the job.

When the Lincolns arrived at the theater at eight o'clock that night, the audience applauded and the orchestra played "Hail to the Chief." After this warm greeting, the president and Mrs. Lincoln sat down to enjoy the show. The evening had gotten off to a wonderful start.

Even Officer Parker was enjoying himself. In the middle of the play, he left the presidential box. President Lincoln seemed fine, the officer thought, so what harm would there be in taking a break for a short drink. As he went out, Officer Parker left the door to the presidential box unlocked.

Toward the end of the play, the door opened and a man entered and walked right up behind the president. Nobody turned around. They were all paying close attention to the play. If any of them heard the man enter, they probably thought he was Officer Parker. But he wasn't.

Suddenly, the man pulled out a gun and fired a shot. President Lincoln slumped down with a bullet wound in the back of his head. Mary screamed. The Lincolns' friend, Major Henry Rathbone, tried to stop the assassin, but the man was too quick. He stabbed the major in the arm and jumped onto the stage.

When the man yelled, "The South shall be free," some people recognized him as the actor, John Wilkes Booth. "Stop that man! Stop that man," yelled the president's friends. Somebody else screamed, "The president is shot." In the confusion, John Wilkes Booth escaped from the theater. Mr. Booth was a Confederate sympathizer who had shot the president in order to get revenge for the South's defeat. He was eventually hunted down and killed by government forces.

Meanwhile, a doctor named Charles Leale made his way through the audience to the presidential box. By that time, Lincoln was unconscious and barely breathing. Dr. Leale realized that there was no hope for the president. "His wound is mortal," the doctor said sadly. "It is impossible for him to recover." The only thing they could do was make President Lincoln more comfortable, so they carried him to a house across the street.

*John Wilkes Booth aiming his gun at
President Lincoln at Ford's Theater*

When Robert Lincoln heard that his father had been shot, he rushed to the house across from Ford's Theater. All night Robert, Mary, and many friends waited by Lincoln's bedside, hoping that he would regain consciousness.

But Doctor Leale had been right. The president would not recover. At 7:22 in the morning on April 15, 1865, Abraham Lincoln died.

FOR
FURTHER READING

OTHER CHILDREN'S
BIOGRAPHIES OF LINCOLN

D'Aulaire, Ingri, and Edgar Parin. *Abraham Lincoln*. New York: Doubleday, 1957.

Horgan, Paul. *Citizen of New Salem*. New York: Farrar, Straus and Giroux, 1961.

Kelly, Regina Z. *Lincoln and Douglas: The Years of Decision*. New York: Random House, 1954.

Miers, Earl Schenk, and Paul M. Angle. *Abraham Lincoln in Peace and War*. New York: American Heritage, 1964.

Sandburg, Carl. *Lincoln Grows Up*. New York: Harcourt, Brace, 1931.

BOOKS ON THE
HISTORY OF THE PERIOD

Athearn, Robert G. *The Civil War*. Vol. 8 of *The American Heritage New Illustrated History of the United States*. New York: Dell, 1963.

————. *The Frontier*. Vol. 6 of *The American Heritage New Illustrated History of the United States*. New York: Dell, 1963.

Catton, Bruce. *The Battle of Gettysburg*. New York: American Heritage, 1963.

Ingraham, Leonard W. *Slavery in the United States*. New York: Franklin Watts, 1968.

Lawson, Don. *The United States in the Civil War*. New York: Abelard-Schuman/Harper & Row, 1977.

Levenson, Dorothy. *The Civil War*, revised edition. New York: Franklin Watts, 1977.

INDEX

*Italicized page numbers
refer to illustrations.*

Abolitionists, 38–39, 47, 48
American Revolution, 22
Anderson, Major Robert,
    58–59
Antietam Creek, Maryland,
    Battle of, 67, 72
Appomattox Courthouse,
    Virginia, 82
Armstrong, Jack, 34–35
Atlanta, Georgia, 78

Baltimore, Maryland, 56, 61
Baton Rouge, Louisiana, 29
Bell, John, 52

Booth, John Wilkes, 84, *85*
Breckenridge, John C., 52
Brooks, Noah, 79
Bull Run River, Virginia,
    Battle of, 63

Civil War, 61–62, 66–67, *68,*
    70, 73, 76, 77, 78–80, 82
Clary Grove Boys, 34–35
Confederate States of
    America, 55–56, 58–59, 61–
    63, 66–67, 70, 73, 76, 78, 80
Congress, U.S., 48
Constitution, U.S., 48, 52,
    Lincoln's proposed
    amendment to, 76
Crook, George, 83

Davis, Jefferson, 55, 80, 82
Democratic party, 52
Dilworth's Spelling Book, 22
Douglas, Senator Stephen
   A., 50–52
Douglass, Frederick, 78

Edwards, Elizabeth, 42–43
Edwards, Ninian, 42–43
Emancipation Proclamation,
   67, 69, 70, 71, 76

Ford's Theater, Washington,
   D.C., 83, 85, 87
Fort Sumter, Charleston,
   South Carolina, 58–59,
   60, 61

Gentry, Allen, 29–31
Gentry, James, 25, 28–29
Gettysburg, Pennsylvania,
   Battle of, 70, 73
Gettysburg Address, 73, 74
Globe Tavern, Springfield,
   Illinois, 44–45
Grant, General Ulysses S.,
   73, 76, 80, 82

Hanks, Dennis, 18–19, 21,
   25, 33
Hill, Ward Lamon, 56

Illinois, 31–32, 36, 50–51
Indiana territory, 16–17, 26,
   28, 31

Johnston, John, 33

Kansas-Nebraska Act, 50
Keckley, Elizabeth, 66–67
Kentucky, 13–14, 17, 20–21, 26

Leale, Dr. Charles, 84, 87
Lee, General Robert E., 67,
   70, 73, 78, 80
Life of Washington
   (Weems), 22
Lincoln, Abraham
      assassination, 85, 87
      birth and childhood, 11,
         13–14, 15, 16–22, 25–26
      campaign for U.S.
         Senate, 50–52
      in Congress, 44–45
      education, 16, 21–22,
         23
      honesty, 35–36
      in Ilinois legislature,
         36–42
      legal career, 37
      marriage, 43
      President, 52–53, 56,
         57, 73, 78

Lincoln, Edward (son), 44–46
Lincoln, Mary Todd (wife), 42–43, *54*, 64, 66–67, 83–84, 87
Lincoln, Nancy Hanks (mother), 14, 18–20
Lincoln, Robert Todd (son), 44–45, 87
Lincoln, Sally Johnston (stepmother), 21–22, 32–33
Lincoln, Sarah (sister), 16, 20–21
Lincoln, Tad (son), 46, 64, *65*, 66, 80
Lincoln, Thomas (father), 14, 16–17, 19–22, 28, 31–33
Lincoln, Willie (son), 46, 64, 66
Lincoln Memorial, *12*

Manassas, Virginia, 62
Mississippi River, 29–31

New Orleans, Louisiana, 29–31, 33–34
New Salem, Illinois, 33–34, 36, 40

Offutt, Denton, 33–34, 36
Owen, Mary, 40–41

Parker, John, 83–84
Pigeon Creek, Indiana, 17–18, 20, 25–26, 28

Rathbone, Major Henry, 84
Republican party, 50–52, 66
Richmond, Virginia, 66, 73, 78, 80, *81*, 82

Sangamon River, 33, 35
Slavery, 13–14, 17, 29–31, 37–39, 42, 45, 47–48, 49, 50–53, 55, 58, 66–67, 76
Sparrow, Elizabeth, 18–19
Sparrow, Thomas, 18–19
Speed, Joshua, 41–42
Springfield, Ilinois, 41–42, 44–47, 55
Stanton, Secretary of War Edwin, 79, 82

Turner, Nat, 38

Union, the, 58, 61, 63, 66–67, 70, 73, 78, 80

Vandalia, Illinois, 36

Washington, George, 22
Washington, D.C., 44–45, 61, 82

ABOUT
THE AUTHOR

Larry Metzger lives in Connecticut with his wife, Elizabeth Alexander, and their dog, Alice Woodruff. In addition to writing, he enjoys basketball, hiking, model railroading, and miniature golf. He has a Ph.D. in history and has taught at both the university and secondary school levels. He currently works as an educational writer and consultant.

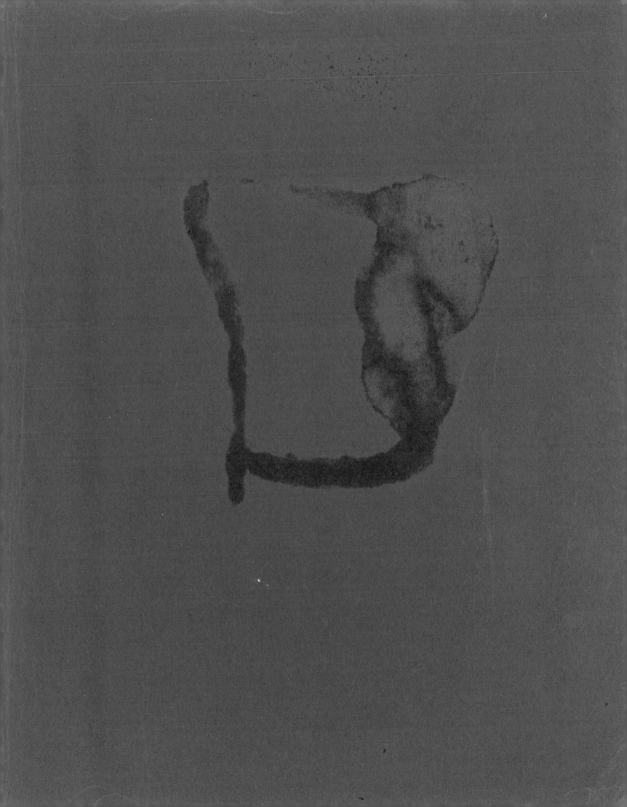

jB   Metzger, Larry
Lincoln   Abraham Lincoln